LEE EVANS ARRANGES

Inspirational Songs

ISBN 0-7935-1924-1

Hal Leonard Publishing Corporation

7777 West Bluemound Road P.O. Box 13819 Milwaukee, WI 53213

LEE EVANS ARRANGES

Inspirational Songs

Contents

I NEED THEE EVERY HOUR

Arranged by
LEE EVANS

JUST A CLOSER WALK WITH THEE

Arranged by
LEE EVANS

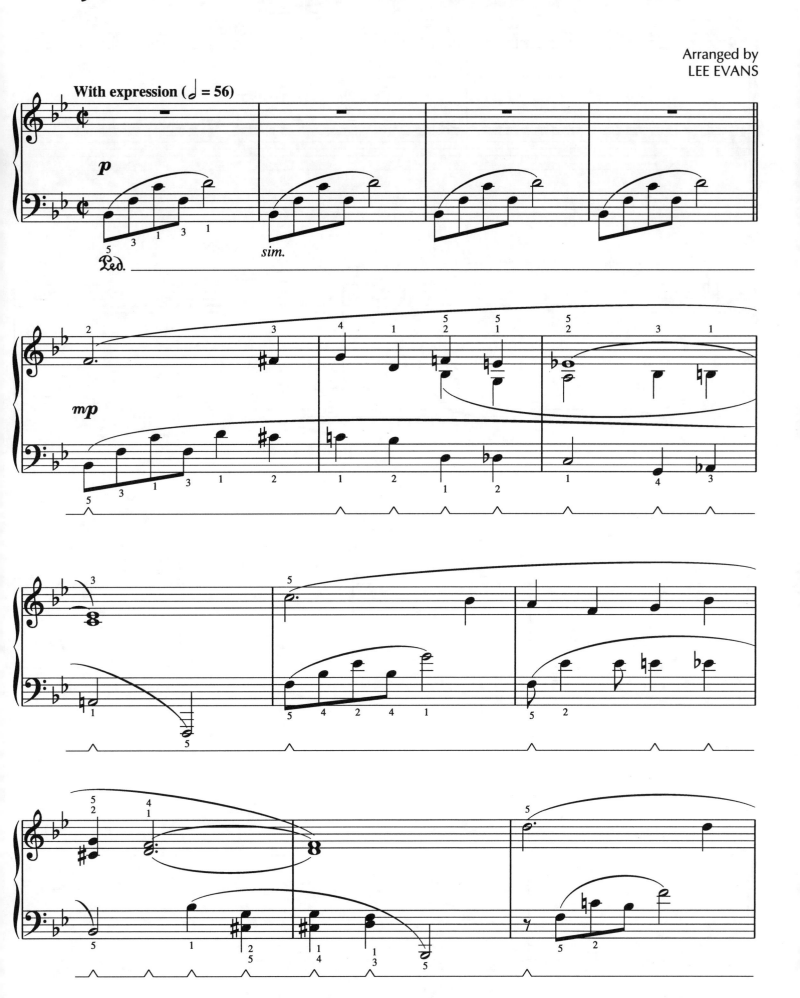

WHAT A FRIEND WE HAVE IN JESUS

Arranged by
LEE EVANS

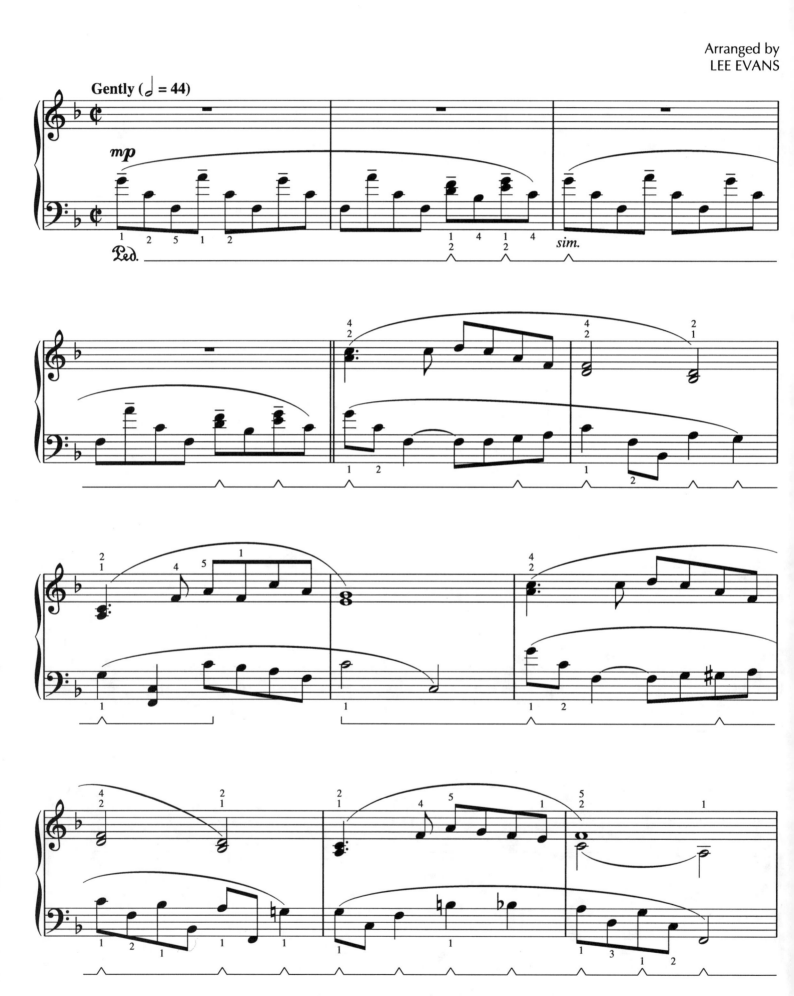

To Coda ⊕

D.C. al Coda

CODA

ETERNAL FATHER, STRONG TO SAVE

Arranged by
LEE EVANS

rit.　　　　a tempo

AMAZING GRACE

Arranged by
LEE EVANS

Slow gospel feel (♩ = 72)

*A broken phrase line gives visual logic to a phrase
containing rests or staccatos.

NOBODY KNOWS THE TROUBLE I'VE SEEN

Arranged by
LEE EVANS

To Coda ⊕

D.S. al Coda

CODA

SOMETIMES I FEEL
LIKE A MOTHERLESS CHILD

Arranged by
LEE EVANS

STAND UP, STAND UP FOR JESUS

Arranged by
LEE EVANS

THE OLD RUGGED CROSS
(On A Far Hill Away)

Arranged by
LEE EVANS

ALL MY TRIALS

Arranged by
LEE EVANS

With spirit (♩ = 84)

(No pedal throughout)

To Coda ⊕

GIMME THAT OLD TIME RELIGION

Arranged by
LEE EVANS

WHEN THE ROLL IS
CALLED UP YONDER

Arranged by
LEE EVANS